SAFETY
SMARTS

SAFE ON THE

SCHOOL BUS

PowerKiDS
press
New York

ROSEMARY JENNINGS

Published in 2017 by The Rosen Publishing Group, Inc.
29 East 21st Street, New York, NY 10010

First Edition

Editor: Theresa Morlock
Book Design: Reann Nye

Photo Credits: Cover (background), p. 24 (bus) Dan Kosmayer/Shutterstock.com; cover (boy) Andy Dean Photography/Shutterstock.com; p. 5 Susan Chiang/E+/Getty Images; pp. 6, 17, 18 Hero Images/Getty Images; p. 9 Sean Locke Photography/Shutterstock.com; p. 10 Hurst Photo/Shutterstock.com; pp. 13 wavebreakmedia/Shutterstock.com; pp. 14, 24 (driver) Monkey Business Images/Shutterstock.com; p. 21 Vstock/Getty Images; p. 22 © iStockphoto.com/Agnieszka Szymczak.

Library of Congress Cataloging-in-Publication Data

Names: Jennings, Rosemary.
Title: Safe on the school bus / Rosemary Jennings.
Description: New York : PowerKids Press, 2017. | Series: Safety smarts |
  Includes index.
Identifiers: LCCN 2016029101| ISBN 9781499427868 (pbk. book) | ISBN
  9781499428667 (6 pack) | ISBN 9781499429923 (library bound book)
Subjects: LCSH: School children–Transportation–Safety measures–Juvenile
  literature. | School buses–Safety measures–Juvenile literature.
Classification: LCC LB2864 J46 2017 | DDC 371.8/72–dc23
LC record available at https://lccn.loc.gov/2016029101

Manufactured in the United States of America

CPSIA Compliance Information: Batch #BW17PK: For Further Information contact Rosen Publishing, New York, New York at 1-800-237-9932

CONTENTS

We wait for the school **bus**.

6

So do our friends.

We are safe on the bus.

9

We stay in our seats.

We keep our hands inside.

13

14

Always listen to the **driver**.

Being loud bothers the driver.

17

18

We stand up only when the bus stops.

Pushing can hurt others.

21

It's time for school!

WORDS TO KNOW

bus

driver

INDEX

WEBSITES

Due to the changing nature of Internet links, PowerKids Press has developed an online list of websites related to the subject of this book. This site is updated regularly. Please use this link to access the list: www.powerkidslinks.com/safe/sbus